THE 30TH BIRTHDAY TRIVIA BOOK

Scott Matthews

CONTENT

INTRODUCTION

Turning 30 is a milestone that feels both exciting and surreal. It's the age where you start to look back and realize just how much you've experienced, while also recognizing how much life is still ahead of you. You've lived through a time of incredible change, from the early days of the internet to a world where everything is instant, connected, and always within reach.

Think about it. You grew up during a unique era, one that bridged two completely different worlds. You remember life before smartphones, when you had to wait your turn on the family computer, burn CDs, or message friends on MSN. Then, almost overnight, everything changed. Social media took over, streaming replaced physical media, and the way we communicate, work, and entertain ourselves was transformed.

This book is a celebration of that journey. It's filled with questions that tap into the moments, trends, and cultural shifts that defined your childhood, teenage years, and early adulthood. Some questions will feel easy, bringing instant answers to mind. Others might make you pause, dig into your memory, and smile when it finally clicks.

More than anything, this book is designed to bring back memories. The songs you had on repeat, the shows you couldn't miss, the trends you followed, and the moments you shared with friends and family. It's a reminder that while the world has changed rapidly, those experiences are what truly define your story.

HOW TO USE THIS BOOK

There's no single way to use this book, and that's part of the fun. You can go through it on your own and test how much you remember, keeping score as you go and seeing how well you really know the last 30 years. Some chapters might feel easier than others, depending on what you paid attention to growing up, which makes it even more interesting.

It also works perfectly as a group activity. Bring it out at a birthday party, a dinner, or a casual get-together and turn it into a game. You can play individually, in teams, or simply take turns answering questions and seeing who remembers the most. It's a great way to spark conversations, share stories, and relive moments that everyone remembers differently.

Each chapter focuses on a different aspect of life, from music and movies to technology, sports, and pop culture. As you move through the book, you'll notice how each section brings back a different type of memory, sometimes something you hadn't thought about in years.

At the end of the book, you'll find bonus pages that shift the focus from trivia to reflection. These pages give you the chance to write down your own memories, experiences, and milestones. Instead of just answering questions, you get to create something personal, turning this book into a snapshot of your life at 30.

There's no pressure to get everything right and no rules you have to follow. Whether you treat it like a challenge, a game, or simply a nostalgic journey, the goal is simple: enjoy it and remember just how much you've lived through.

CHAPTER 1

The Early 90s (1990-1995)

The early 1990s marked a transformative period where technology was just beginning to reshape daily life, yet the world still felt analog in many ways. This was the era of grunge music, dial-up internet sounds, and the birth of the World Wide Web, a time when you actually had to plan to watch your favorite show or risk missing it forever. Blockbuster Video dominated Friday nights, Game Boys kept us entertained during long car rides, and the biggest social drama happened face-to-face or over landline phones. The early 90s captured a unique moment in history: the last generation to grow up without smartphones, yet the first to experience the early internet's wild, unfiltered chaos.

1. Which TV network launched in 1993 and quickly became known for shows like Beavis and Butt-Head?

a) Nickelodeon
b) MTV
c) Cartoon Network
d) Fox Kids

2. What was the name of the social network that featured the "Top 8" friends list?

a) Friendster
b) MySpace
c) Orkut
d) Bebo

3. Which company created the Windows operating system that became widely used in the early 1990s?

a) Apple
b) IBM
c) Microsoft
d) Intel

4. Which Disney film released in 1994 became one of the highest-grossing animated movies of all time?

a) Aladdin
b) The Lion King
c) Beauty and the Beast
d) Pocahontas

5. Which grunge band released the album "Nevermind" in 1991?

a. Pearl Jam
b. Soundgarden
c. Nirvana
d. Alice in Chains

6. What was the name of the animated sitcom that debuted in 1989 but became hugely popular in the early 1990s?

a. South Park
b. The Simpsons
c. Futurama
d. King of the Hill

7. Which fast-food chain introduced the "Where's the Beef?" advertising campaign in the 1980s but remained popular in the early 1990s?

a. Wendy's
b. McDonald's
c. Burger King
d. Taco Bell

8. What was the name of the first Pixar animated feature film released in 1995?

a. A Bug's Life
b. Toy Story
c. Monsters, Inc.
d. Finding Nemo

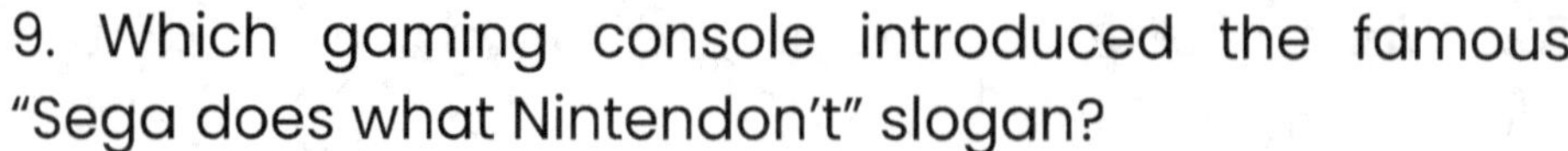

9. Which gaming console introduced the famous "Sega does what Nintendon't" slogan?

a) Sega Genesis
b) Sega Saturn
c) Atari Jaguar
d) Neo Geo

10. What was the name of the first PlayStation console released by Sony in 1994?

a. PlayStation 1
b. PS One
c. PlayStation
d. Sega Saturn

11. Which sitcom, featuring a group of friends in New York, premiered in 1994?

a. Seinfeld
b. Friends
c. Cheers
d. Frasier

12. What was the name of the coffee beverage that became a major trend in the early 1990s?

a. Espresso
b. Cappuccino
c. Latte
d. Mocha

13. Which Olympic Games took place in 1992?

a. Barcelona Summer Olympics
b. Albertville Winter Olympics
c. Both A and B
d. Neither A nor B

14. What was the name of the social movement that emerged in the early 1990s focusing on environmental conservation?

a. Environmentalism
b. Eco-consciousness
c. Green movement
d. Sustainability

15. Which technology company released the PowerBook laptop in 1991?

a. IBM
b. Compaq
c. Apple
d. Dell

16. What was the name of the popular teen magazine that launched in 1994?

a. Seventeen
b. Teen People
c. YM Magazine
d. Twist

17. Which movie starring Jim Carrey was released in 1994 and became a massive hit?

a. Dumb and Dumber
b. The Mask
c. Ace Ventura: Pet Detective
d. Liar Liar

18. What was the name of the first widely used web browser released in 1993?

a) Netscape Navigator
b) Internet Explorer
c) Mosaic
d) Opera

19. Which British rock band released the album "Definitely Maybe" in 1994?

a. Blur
b. Oasis
c. Pulp
d. Suede

20. What was the name of the first search engine that became widely used on the internet?

a. Yahoo
b. AltaVista
c. Lycos
d. Excite

1. c) Cartoon Network – Cartoon Network launched in 1992 (early 90s) and quickly became known for airing classic cartoons and original shows, becoming a major part of kids' entertainment.

2. c) WorldWideWeb - Tim Berners-Lee released the first web browser in 1991, making the World Wide Web accessible to the general public for the first time.

3. c) Microsoft – Windows 3.0 and later versions helped Microsoft dominate personal computing in the early 90s.

4. b) The Lion King – Released in 1994, it became a massive global success and remains one of Disney's most iconic films.

5. c) Nirvana - Kurt Cobain and Nirvana's "Nevermind" became the defining album of the grunge era and changed rock music forever with its raw authenticity.

6. b) The Simpsons - "The Simpsons" debuted in 1989 but became a massive hit in the early 1990s and remains on the air today as the longest-running animated series.

7. a) Wendy's - Wendy's "Where's the Beef?" campaign became iconic in the 1980s and remained popular into the early 1990s as a memorable advertising moment.

8. b) Toy Story – "Toy Story" revolutionized animation and launched the Pixar empire that continues to dominate family entertainment to this day.

9. a) Sega Genesis – Sega used this slogan to market the Genesis against Nintendo in the early 90s.

10. c) PlayStation – The original PlayStation revolutionized gaming and competed successfully against Nintendo and Sega in the 1990s with superior graphics and processing power.

11. b) Friends – "Friends" premiered in 1994 and became one of the most popular and influential sitcoms of all time, defining a generation.

12. b) Cappuccino – Espresso-based drinks like cappuccino and latte became major trends in the early 1990s as coffee culture exploded in America.

13. c) Both A and B – The 1992 Barcelona Summer Olympics and Albertville Winter Olympics both took place in 1992, making it an Olympic year.

14. a) Environmentalism – Environmentalism, eco-consciousness, and the green movement all emerged as major social movements in the early 1990s.

15. c) Apple – Apple released the PowerBook laptop in 1991, which became hugely influential in the design of modern laptops with its innovative trackpad.

16. b) Teen People – Teen People magazine launched in 1998 and became hugely popular among teenagers in the late 1990s with celebrity news and trends.

17. a) Dumb and Dumber – Jim Carrey's "Dumb and Dumber" became a massive hit and

19. b) Oasis - Oasis' "Definitely Maybe" became one of the best-selling debut albums of all time and defined the Britpop movement.

20. b) AltaVista - AltaVista was one of the first widely used search engines before Google revolutionized the industry with better search algorithms.

The early 1990s quietly launched the internet, but almost no one was using it yet. The World Wide Web was introduced in 1991, but it remained mostly limited to scientists and universities. The first widely used browser, Mosaic, didn't appear until 1993, and even then, most people had never seen a website.

In 1994, online shopping began with a surprisingly simple purchase, a Sting CD sold through NetMarket. At the time, entering your credit card details online felt risky and unfamiliar, and many people doubted it would ever catch on. Yet this small moment marked the beginning of a global shift, paving the way for companies like Amazon and completely changing how we buy everything from books to groceries today.

Music in the early 90s didn't just evolve, it flipped the culture overnight. When "Smells Like Teen Spirit" by Nirvana exploded in 1991, it signaled the end of the polished, glamorous sound of the 1980s. Grunge brought a raw, emotional energy that resonated with young people, influencing not just music but fashion, attitudes, and identity. Flannel shirts, ripped jeans, and an anti-establishment mindset became symbols of a generation pushing back against the excess of the decade before.

Sports Champions & Moments

Sports have always been a universal language that transcends borders, cultures, and generations. From the moment we're old enough to hold a ball, we're captivated by the drama, the triumph, and the heartbreak that comes with athletic competition. The greatest athletes become more than just players, they become cultural icons, symbols of excellence, and sources of inspiration for millions of people around the world. Whether it's a perfect game, an impossible comeback, or a record-breaking performance, sports moments have a way of defining entire eras and bringing people together in ways that few other things can.

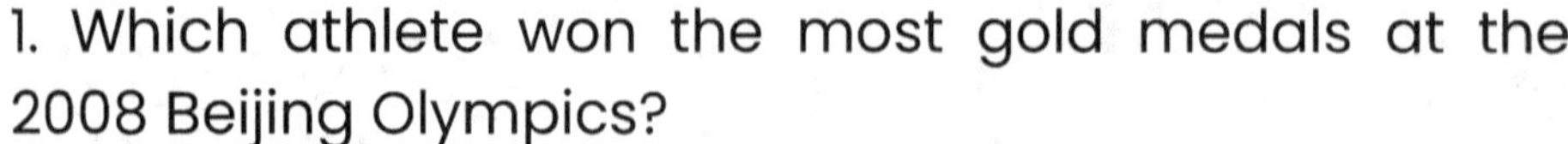

1. Which athlete won the most gold medals at the 2008 Beijing Olympics?

a. Usain Bolt
b. Michael Phelps
c. Simone Biles
d. Serena Williams

2. In what year did the New England Patriots win their first Super Bowl?

a. 1999
b. 2001
c. 2003
d. 2005

3. Which tennis player won the most Grand Slam titles in the 2010s?

a. Novak Djokovic
b. Rafael Nadal
c. Roger Federer
d. Andy Murray

4. What year did LeBron James win his first NBA championship?

a. 2010
b. 2011
c. 2012
d. 2013

5. Which soccer player won the most Ballon d'Or awards?

a. Cristiano Ronaldo
b. Lionel Messi
c. Pelé
d. Diego Maradona

6. In what year did the Golden State Warriors win 73 games in a single NBA season?

a. 2014
b. 2015
c. 2016
d. 2017

7. Which athlete became the first woman to win an Olympic gold medal in skateboarding?

a. Erin Jackson
b. Momiji Nishiya
c. Aly Raisman
d. Simone Biles

8. What year did Tom Brady retire from the NFL?

a. 2022
b. 2023
c. 2024
d. 2025

9. Which boxer defeated Floyd Mayweather Jr. in a professional boxing match?

a. Manny Pacquiao
b. Canelo Alvarez
c. No one (he retired undefeated)
d. Conor McGregor

10. In what year did Serena Williams win her 23rd Grand Slam title?

a. 2016
b. 2017
c. 2018
d. 2019

11. Which team won the 2023 Super Bowl?

a. Kansas City Chiefs
b. San Francisco 49ers
c. Philadelphia Eagles
d. Dallas Cowboys

12. What year did Usain Bolt retire from professional track and field?

a. 2015
b. 2016
c. 2017
d. 2018

13. Which athlete won the most Olympic gold medals of all time?

a. Michael Phelps
b. Larisa Latynina
c. Nikolay Andrianov
d. Simone Biles

14. In what year did the Los Angeles Lakers win their 17th NBA championship?

a. 2019
b. 2020
c. 2021
d. 2022

15. Which athlete won the most Wimbledon singles titles?

a. Roger Federer
b. Pete Sampras
c. Novak Djokovic
d. Rafael Nadal

16. What year did Tiger Woods win his first Masters Tournament?

a. 1995
b. 1997
c. 1999
d. 2001

17. Which team won the 2016 NBA Championship?

a. Golden State Warriors
b. Cleveland Cavaliers
c. Oklahoma City Thunder
d. San Antonio Spurs

18. In what year did Muhammad Ali pass away?

a. 2014
b. 2016
c. 2018
d. 2020

19. Which female athlete won the most Olympic medals?

a. Simone Biles
b. Larisa Latynina
c. Valentina Tereshkova
d. Nadia Comaneci

20. What year did the Chicago Cubs win the World Series for the first time in 108 years?

a. 2014
b. 2015
c. 2016
d. 2017

CHAPTER 2 ANSWERS

1. b) Michael Phelps - Michael Phelps won 8 gold medals at the 2008 Beijing Olympics, setting an Olympic record that stood until the 2016 Rio Olympics.

2. b) 2001 - The New England Patriots won Super Bowl XXXVI in February 2002 (for the 2001 season), marking the beginning of their dynasty.

3. a) Novak Djokovic - Novak Djokovic won 12 Grand Slam titles during the 2010s, dominating men's tennis during that decade with consistency.

4. c) 2012 - LeBron James won his first NBA championship with the Miami Heat in 2012, defeating the Oklahoma City Thunder in the Finals.

5. b) Lionel Messi - Lionel Messi won 8 Ballon d'Or awards, more than any other player in history, cementing his legacy as one of football's greatest.

6. c) 2016 - The Golden State Warriors won 73 games in the 2015-2016 season, breaking the previous record of 72 set by the Chicago Bulls.

7. b) Momiji Nishiya - From Japan, she became the first woman to win an Olympic gold medal in skateboarding at the 2020 Tokyo Olympics (held in 2021), winning the street competition at just 13 years old.

8. b) 2023 - Tom Brady retired from the NFL in February 2022, then unretired briefly before retiring again in 2023 after an incredible career.

9. c) No one (he retired undefeated) - Floyd Mayweather Jr. retired with a perfect 50-0 record, never losing a professional boxing match in his career.

10. b) 2017 - Serena Williams won her 23rd Grand Slam title at the 2017 Australian Open while pregnant with her daughter, showing incredible strength.

11. a) Kansas City Chiefs - The Kansas City Chiefs defeated the Philadelphia Eagles in Super Bowl LVII in February 2023 with a dominant performance.

12. c) 2017 - Usain Bolt retired after the 2017 World Championships in London, ending his legendary track and field career with grace.

13. a) Michael Phelps - Michael Phelps won 23 Olympic gold medals, more than any other athlete in Olympic history, a record that may never be broken.

14. b) 2020 - The Los Angeles Lakers won the NBA championship in 2020 (for the 2019-2020 season) in the bubble in Orlando during the pandemic.

15. a) Roger Federer - Roger Federer won 8 Wimbledon singles titles, more than any other male player in history at that time.

16. b) 1997 - Tiger Woods won his first Masters Tournament in 1997 at age 21, becoming the youngest Masters champion ever.

17. b) Cleveland Cavaliers - The Cleveland Cavaliers defeated the Golden State Warriors in the 2016 NBA Finals, winning the city's first championship.

18. b) 2016 - Muhammad Ali passed away on June 3, 2016, at the age of 74, leaving behind an incredible legacy in boxing and activism.

19. b) Larisa Latynina - Larisa Latynina won 18 Olympic medals as a Soviet gymnast, holding the record until Michael Phelps surpassed it.

20. c) 2016 - The Chicago Cubs won the World Series in 2016, ending a 108-year drought and bringing the championship to Chicago.

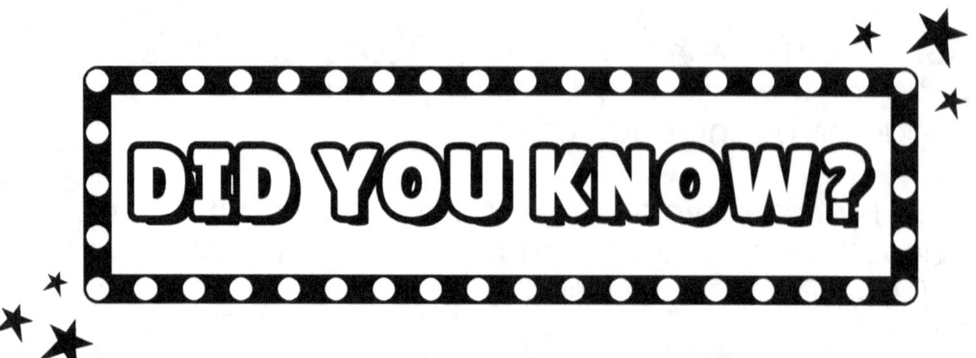

At the 2000 Sydney Olympics, Cathy Freeman became the first Aboriginal Australian to light the Olympic cauldron, a historic moment of reconciliation and cultural significance. Freeman then went on to win the gold medal in the 400 meters, becoming a national hero and symbol of progress. Her victory was watched by over 3.7 billion people worldwide, making Sydney 2000 one of the most-watched sporting events in history and proving the transformative power of sport to unite nations and inspire change.

In 2016, Usain Bolt completed an incredible "triple-triple" at the Olympics—winning gold in the 100m, 200m, and 4x100m relay for the third consecutive Games. No sprinter had ever dominated across three Olympics like that before, cementing Bolt as the fastest and most dominant track athlete of all time.

In 2019, Eliud Kipchoge became the first person in history to run a marathon in under two hours, finishing in 1:59:40. Although it wasn't officially recognized as a world record due to controlled conditions, it proved that what was once thought impossible could be achieved, redefining the limits of human endurance.

The Late 90s (1996-1999)

The late 1990s represented the final chapter of the pre-smartphone era, a moment when the digital revolution was beginning but hadn't yet made everyone constantly connected. This was the era of Tamagotchis, pog collections, and the Spice Girls, a time when boy bands ruled the charts, teen magazines were essential reading, and the biggest social events happened at the mall or at sleepovers. The late 90s had an optimistic energy, a sense that the future was bright and full of possibility. The economy was booming, technology was advancing rapidly, and there was a palpable excitement about what the new millennium would bring.

1. Which boy band sang "I Want It That Way" in 1999?

a. *NSYNC
b. Backstreet Boys
c. New Kids on the Block
d. 98 Degrees

2. What was the name of the coffee shop in the TV show "Friends"?

a. Java Joe's
b. Central Perk
c. The Daily Grind
d. Brew Haven

3. Which movie won the Academy Award for Best Picture in 1998?

a. Titanic
b. The Full Monty
c. Good Will Hunting
d. As Good as It Gets

4. Which globally popular 1990s dance trend, driven by a Spanish duo's hit song, featured a sequence of synchronized arm movements and became a staple at parties, weddings, and sporting events?

a. The Hustle
b. The Macarena
c. The Cha-Cha Slide
d. The Cupid Shuffle

5. Which Spice Girl was known as "Posh Spice"?

a. Melanie C
b. Emma Brown
c. Victoria Beckham
d. Melanie B

6. What was the name of the dial-up internet service that dominated the late 1990s?

a. CompuServe
b. AOL (America Online)
c. Prodigy
d. Earthlink

7. Which British girl group had a hit with "Wannabe" in 1996?

a. All Saints
b. Spice Girls
c. Steps
d. Atomic Kitten

8. Which major event in 1999 was often referred to as the "Y2K bug" concern?

a) Internet crash
b) Calendar reset issue
c) Computer date error
d) Software virus outbreak

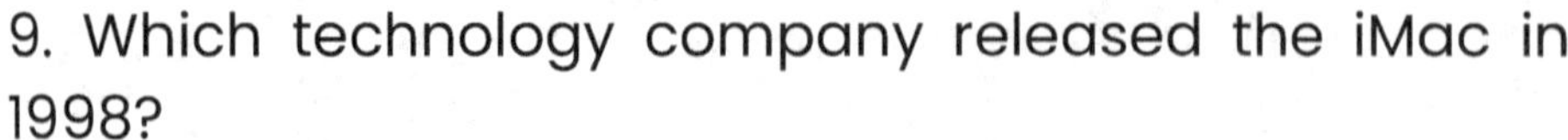

9. Which technology company released the iMac in 1998?

a. IBM
b. Compaq
c. Apple
d. Dell

10. What was the name of the popular teen magazine that launched in 1998?

a. Seventeen
b. Teen People
c. YM Magazine
d. Twist

11. Which animated sitcom, created by Matt Groening, became a massive hit in the late 1990s?

a. South Park
b. The Simpsons
c. Futurama
d. King of the Hill

12. Which reality TV show, set in a shared house with strangers, helped define the genre's early popularity in the late 1990s?

a. Survivor
b. The Real World
c. Fear Factor
d. American Idol

13. Which movie starring Jim Carrey was released in 1994 but remained popular throughout the late 1990s?

a. Dumb and Dumber
b. The Mask
c. Ace Ventura: Pet Detective
d. Liar Liar

14. In which year was Pokémon Blue first released internationally, helping spark a global gaming phenomenon?

a. 1996
b. 1997
c. 1998
d. 1999

15. Which fashion trend became hugely popular in the late 1990s among teenagers?

a. Cargo pants
b. Platform shoes
c. Baby tees
d. Slip dresses

16. Which boy band released the album Millennium in 1999, becoming one of the best-selling albums of all time?

a) NSYNC
b) Backstreet Boys
c) 98 Degrees
d) Westlife

17. Which 1997 blockbuster became the highest-grossing film of all time upon its release?

a. Titanic
b. The Lost World: Jurassic Park
c. The Fifth Element
d. Batman & Robin

18. What was the name of the popular video streaming service that launched in 1997?

a. Netflix
b. Blockbuster Online
c. Amazon Prime Video
d. Hulu

19. Which British rock band released "OK Computer" in 1997?

a. Blur
b. Oasis
c. Radiohead
d. Pulp

20. What was the name of the first webcam that became commercially available?

a. Logitech QuickCam
b. Creative WebCam
c. Microsoft LifeCam
d. Razer Kiyo

CHAPTER 3 ANSWERS

1. b) Backstreet Boys - The Backstreet Boys' "I Want It That Way" became one of the most iconic boy band songs of the 1990s and a cultural touchstone.

2. b) Central Perk - The coffee shop served as the central gathering place for the six main characters throughout the show's 10-season run.

3. a) Titanic - James Cameron's "Titanic" became a cultural phenomenon and won 11 Academy Awards, tying the record set by "Ben-Hur."

4. b) The Macarena - The song and its accompanying dance became a global phenomenon in 1996-1997, appearing at weddings and parties worldwide.

5. c) Victoria Beckham - Victoria Beckham, later known as Posh Spice, became one of the most recognizable members of the Spice Girls globally.

6. b) AOL (America Online) - AOL's "You've Got Mail" notification became iconic, and the service was the gateway to the internet for millions.

7. b) Spice Girls - The Spice Girls' "Wannabe" launched the group to international stardom and defined girl group pop music of the late 1990s.

8. c) Computer date error – Many feared computers would fail when the year changed from 1999 to 2000 due to date formatting issues.

9. c) Apple - Apple released the iMac in 1998, which revolutionized computer design with its colorful, translucent aesthetic and innovative styling.

10. b) Teen People - Teen People magazine launched in 1998 and became hugely popular among teenagers in the late 1990s with celebrity coverage.

11. b) The Simpsons - "The Simpsons" became a massive hit in the late 1990s and remains one of the longest-running animated series ever created.

12. b) The Real World – "The Real World," which debuted on MTV in 1992, remained hugely popular throughout the late 1990s and is widely credited with helping pioneer modern reality television.

13. d) Liar Liar - Jim Carrey's "Liar Liar" was released in 1997 and became one of his most successful comedies of the decade.

14. c) 1998 – Pokémon Blue was released internationally in 1998, introducing players worldwide to the Pokémon universe and becoming one of the most influential handheld games of all time.

15. a) Cargo pants - Cargo pants became hugely popular fashion trends among teenagers in the late 1990s as casual wear became mainstream.

16. b) Backstreet Boys – Millennium sold millions of copies worldwide and helped define late 90s pop music.

17. a) Titanic - "Titanic" became the highest-grossing film of all time in 1997, surpassing "Jurassic Park" with its epic romance and disaster.

18. a) Netflix - Netflix launched in 1997 as a DVD rental service before transitioning to streaming in the 2000s and revolutionizing entertainment.

19. c) Radiohead - Radiohead's "OK Computer" became one of the most critically acclaimed albums of the 1990s and influenced alternative rock.

20. a) Logitech QuickCam - The Logitech QuickCam was one of the first commercially available webcams for personal computers in the late 1990s.

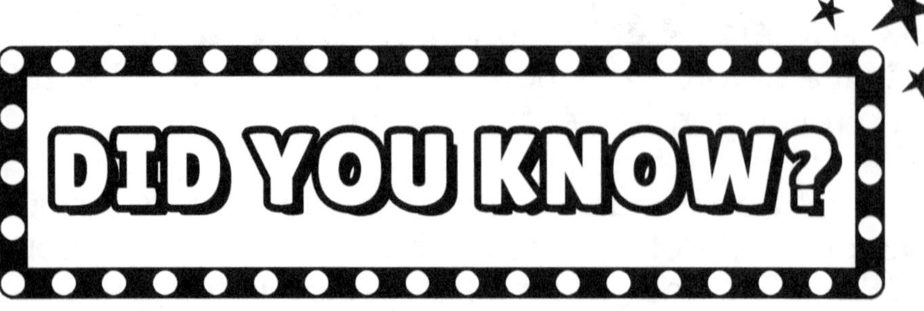

In 1999, Pokémon Red and Blue helped spark a global craze that went far beyond gaming. Kids weren't just playing. They were trading cards at school, watching the TV show after class, and linking Game Boys with cables to battle each other. Some rare Pokémon cards even became so valuable that they were treated like collectibles, with playground trades sometimes turning into serious negotiations.

In 1998, Google was founded by two university students, but almost no one paid attention at the time. Early search engines were cluttered and confusing, while Google's clean homepage looked almost empty by comparison. What made it special was its ability to rank results better than anyone else, quickly turning it into the tool people trusted without even thinking about it.

In 1997, Harry Potter and the Philosopher's Stone by J. K. Rowling was first published in a small print run with approximately 500 copies. Many of those original books ended up in school libraries, and today, first editions can sell for tens of thousands of dollars. What started as a simple story about a young wizard soon grew into one of the biggest entertainment franchises in history.

CHAPTER 4

Music Through The Years

Music has always been the soundtrack to our lives, the art form that captures the spirit of an era and speaks directly to our emotions. From the moment we're born, music surrounds us, it marks our milestones, accompanies our celebrations, and provides solace during our darkest moments. The greatest musicians transcend their time, creating work that resonates across generations and continues to inspire long after they're gone. Whether it's the raw power of rock and roll, the sophistication of jazz, the energy of hip-hop, or the emotional depth of soul music, music has the unique ability to unite people across all boundaries.

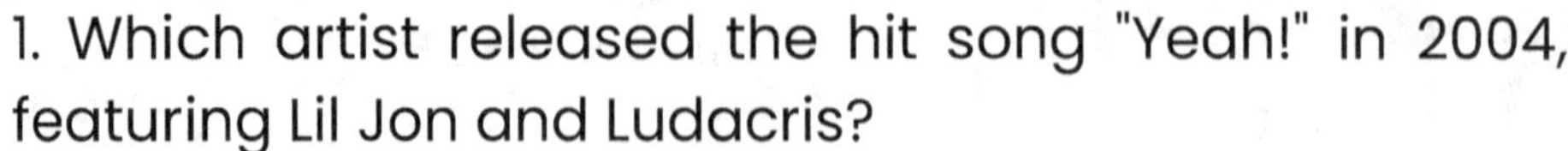

1. Which artist released the hit song "Yeah!" in 2004, featuring Lil Jon and Ludacris?

a. Usher
b. Justin Timberlake
c. Nelly
d. Chris Brown

2. Which British boy band released the hit song "What Makes You Beautiful" in 2011?

a. Take That
b. Westlife
c. One Direction
d. The Wanted

3. Which female artist has won the most Grammy Awards in history?

a. Beyoncé
b. Taylor Swift
c. Aretha Franklin
d. Whitney Houston

4. What was the name of the music festival that took place in August 1969 and became iconic?

a. Monterey Pop Festival
b. Woodstock
c. Newport Folk Festival
d. Coachella

5. Which artist released the hit song "Rolling in the Deep" in 2010?

a. Amy Winehouse
b. Adele
c. Duffy
d. Ellie Goulding

6. What was the name of the first music video ever broadcast on MTV in 1981?

a. Billie Jean
b. Like a Virgin
c. Video Killed the Radio Star
d. Thriller

7. Which artist released the album Good Girl Gone Bad in 2007?

a. Beyoncé
b. Rihanna
c. Ciara
d. Fergie

8. Which member of N.W.A is known for co-founding Beats Electronics, the company behind Beats headphones?

a. Eazy-E
b. Dr. Dre
c. Ice Cube
d. MC Ren

9. Which artist released the album "Like a Prayer" in 1989?

a. Prince
b. Michael Jackson
c. Madonna
d. Janet Jackson

10. Which Britpop band known for "Don't Look Back in Anger," released their debut album Definitely Maybe in 1994?

a. Blur
b. Oasis
c. Pulp
d. Suede

11. Which artist released the 1995 album Jagged Little Pill, featuring hits like "Ironic" and "You Oughta Know"?

a. Alanis Morissette
b. Sheryl Crow
c. Fiona Apple
d. Natalie Imbruglia

12. Which pop artist released the hit single "...Baby One More Time" in 1998, launching a major comeback for teen pop?

a. Christina Aguilera
b. Britney Spears
c. Mandy Moore
d. Jessica Simpson

13. Which artist released the album "Confessions" in 2006?

a. Britney Spears
b. Christina Aguilera
c. Madonna
d. Gwen Stefani

14. What was the name of the album released by Adele in 2011?

a. 19
b. 21
c. 25
d. 30

15. Which artist released the album "Lemonade" in 2016?

a. Rihanna
b. Beyoncé
c. Nicki Minaj
d. Cardi B

16. What was the name of the music streaming service that launched in the United States in 2011?

a. Spotify
b. Apple Music
c. Tidal
d. Amazon Music

17. Which artist released the 2014 album 1989, whose title references the year she was born and which became her first official pop-only record?

a. Ariana Grande
b. Taylor Swift
c. Lorde
d. Katy Perry

18. Which rock band released the album "The Dark Side of the Moon" in 1973?

a. Pink Floyd
b. Led Zeppelin
c. The Who
d. Queen

19. Which artist released the hit song "Blinding Lights" in 2019, which went on to become one of the longest-charting songs in Billboard history?

a. Drake
b. Post Malone
c. The Weeknd
d. Travis Scott

20. What was the name of the final album released by The Beatles in 1969?

a. Abbey Road
b. The White Album
c. Sgt. Pepper's Lonely Hearts Club Band
d. Revolver

CHAPTER 4 ANSWERS

1. a) Usher - "Yeah!" became one of the biggest songs of the 2000s, dominating radio, clubs, and MTV, and is still instantly recognizable to anyone who grew up in that era.

2. c) One Direction - Formed on The X Factor, One Direction became one of the biggest boy bands of the 2010s, with "What Makes You Beautiful" launching their global success.

3. a) Beyoncé - Beyoncé has won over 30 Grammy Awards, more than any other artist in history, cementing her legacy as one of music's greatest performers and most awarded artists.

4. b) Woodstock - Woodstock took place in August 1969 and became one of the most iconic music festivals of all time, defining the counterculture movement and bringing together hundreds of thousands of people.

5. b) Adele - "Rolling in the Deep" was a massive global hit and helped establish Adele as one of the biggest artists of the 2010s, winning multiple awards and dominating charts worldwide.

6. c) "Video Killed the Radio Star" - This was MTV's first music video ever broadcast, launching the music video era and changing how music was consumed forever.

7. b) Rihanna - Good Girl Gone Bad marked a major shift in Rihanna's image and sound, with "Umbrella" becoming the breakout hit that defined her transition into global superstardom.

8. b) Dr. Dre - After his music career, Dr. Dre co-founded Beats by Dre, which became a massive global brand and was later acquired by Apple for billions.

9. c) Madonna - "Like a Prayer" became one of Madonna's most successful albums and sparked controversy with its provocative music video featuring religious imagery.

10. b) Oasis - Definitely Maybe became one of the fastest-selling debut albums in UK history and helped launch Oasis into global fame during the Britpop era.

11. a) Alanis Morissette - Jagged Little Pill became one of the best-selling albums of the 1990s, known for its raw lyrics and massive hits that defined an era of alternative rock and pop.

12. b) Britney Spears – Britney Spears released "...Baby One More Time" in 1998, which became a worldwide hit and helped define late 1990s pop music.

13. c) Madonna - "Confessions" became one of Madonna's most successful albums of the 2000s and showcased her continued relevance and ability to reinvent herself.

14. b) 21 - "21" became one of the best-selling albums of all time and won multiple Grammy Awards for Adele's incredible voice and emotional depth.

15. b) Beyoncé - "Lemonade" was released as a visual album and became one of the most acclaimed albums of the 2010s, showcasing Beyoncé's artistic vision and cultural commentary.

16. a) Spotify – Spotify originally launched in Sweden in 2008 but expanded to the United States in 2011, helping it grow into the world's leading music streaming platform.

17. b) Taylor Swift - The album title 1989 refers to her birth year, and the project marked a deliberate shift away from country into a fully pop sound, redefining her career.

18. a) Pink Floyd - "The Dark Side of the Moon" became one of the best-selling albums of all time and is considered a masterpiece of progressive rock.

19. c) The Weeknd - "Blinding Lights" became a global smash hit, known for its 80s-inspired sound and record-breaking run on the charts, making it one of the biggest songs of the late 2010s.

20. a) Abbey Road - "Abbey Road" was The Beatles' final album released in 1969, featuring iconic tracks like "Come Together" and "Here Comes the Sun."

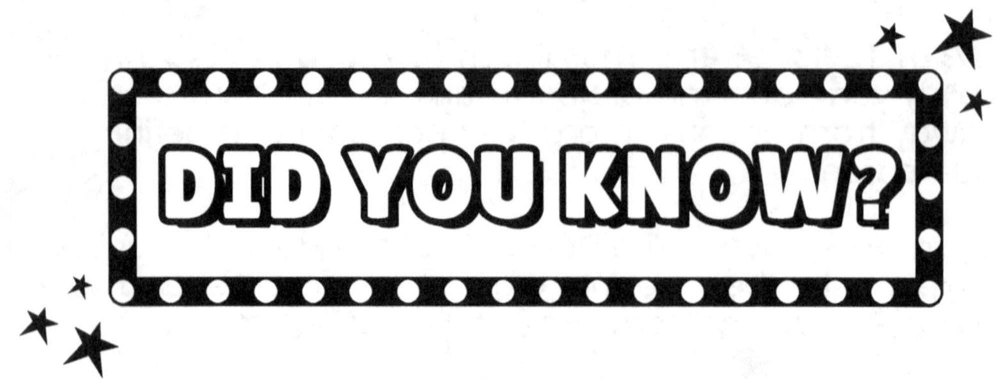

Hidden tracks were a fun surprise in the late 90s and early 2000s. Artists would place secret songs at the end of albums, sometimes after several minutes of silence, rewarding listeners who let the CD keep playing instead of stopping at the final track. Finding one felt like discovering a bonus nobody told you about.

Ringtone music became a massive business in the early 2000s. Before smartphones, people paid to download short clips of songs to customize their phones, and at its peak, ringtone sales generated billions worldwide. Some artists even made more money from ringtones than from the actual song sales.

Some of the biggest songs ever were never expected to be hits. Happy by Pharrell Williams was originally written for a movie soundtrack, yet it went on to top charts in over 20 countries and became one of the most recognizable songs of the 2010s.

CHAPTER 5

The New Millennium

The new millennium arrived with a sense of possibility and wonder. The year 2000 had been anticipated for years. Would computers crash? Would society collapse? When nothing catastrophic happened, there was a collective sigh of relief and a sense that we could move forward into a new era with optimism. The 2000s represented a unique moment in history when technology was advancing rapidly but hadn't yet consumed every aspect of our lives. This was the era of the iPod, the rise of social media, and the beginning of the streaming revolution. It was also the era of reality TV, the Iraq War, and the financial crisis that would reshape the global economy.

1. Which social media platform launched in 2004?

a. MySpace
b. Friendster
c. Facebook
d. Orkut

2. Which video platform revolutionized how people share and consume video content?

a. Vimeo
b. YouTube
c. Dailymotion
d. Metacafe

3. Which musical won the Academy Award for Best Picture in 2003?

a. Chicago
b. Moulin Rouge
c. Hairspray
d. Dreamgirls

4. Which social networking site was the most visited in the world from 2005 to 2008?

a. Facebook
b. Orkut
c. MySpace
d. Friendster

5. Which reality TV show premiered on May 31, 2000, and became hugely successful?

a. American Idol
b. Survivor
c. The Real World
d. Fear Factor

6. What was the storage capacity of the first iPod released in 2001?

a. 512 MB
b. 1 GB
c. 5 GB
d. 10 GB

7. In RuneScape, what was the maximum level a player could achieve in a single skill?

a. 50
b. 99
c. 100
d. 120

8. What are the primary colors used in the classic eBay logo?

a. Red, blue, yellow, green
b. Red, blue, yellow, orange
c. Blue, green, yellow, orange
d. Red, blue, green, purple

9. Which Pixar film, released in 2003, won the Academy Award for Best Animated Feature?

a. Toy Story 2
b. Finding Nemo
c. Monsters, Inc.
d. The Incredibles

10. Which contestant won the first season of "American Idol" in 2002?

a. Justin Guarini
b. Kelly Clarkson
c. Fantasia Barrino
d. Ruben Studdard

11. Which social media platform revolutionized real-time communication?

a. Facebook
b. MySpace
c. Twitter
d. Orkut

12. In what year was the first modern BlackBerry smartphone with calling capabilities (the BlackBerry 5810) released?

a. 2000
b. 2002
c. 2004
d. 2006

13. Which Batman film was released in 2008?

a. The Dark Knight
b. Batman Begins
c. The Dark Knight Rises
d. Batman v Superman: Dawn of Justice

14. Which James Cameron film became a global phenomenon and held the record for highest-grossing film?

a. Titanic
b. Avatar
c. Terminator 2
d. True Lies

15. Which social network was particularly popular in Brazil and India?

a. Friendster
b. MySpace
c. Orkut
d. Hi5

16. Which Tom Hanks film became a massive hit in 2000?

a. Forrest Gump
b. Cast Away
c. Philadelphia
d. Saving Private Ryan

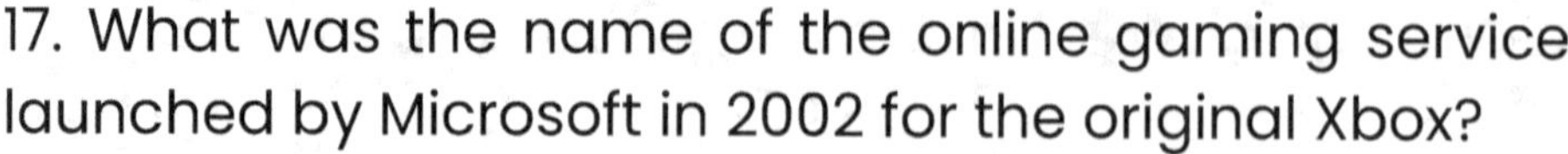

17. What was the name of the online gaming service launched by Microsoft in 2002 for the original Xbox?

a. PlayStation Network
b. Game Pass
c. Xbox Live
d. Xbox Connect

18. In what year was the film 8 Mile released?

a. 2000
b. 2001
c. 2002
d. 2004

19. Which photo-sharing website launched in 2004?

a. Instagram
b. Flickr
c. Picasa
d. Photobucket

20. Which film won the Academy Award for Best Picture in 2009?

a. Slumdog Millionaire
b. The Curious Case of Benjamin Button
c. Iron Man
d. WALL-E

CHAPTER 5 ANSWERS

1. c) Facebook - Facebook launched from Zuckerberg's Harvard dorm room and eventually became the world's largest social media platform, fundamentally changing how people connect.

2. b) YouTube - YouTube revolutionized how people share and consume video content, launching the era of user-generated media and making video accessible to everyone.

3. a) Chicago - "Chicago" became the first musical to win Best Picture in 34 years, reviving interest in the genre and winning multiple Academy Awards.

4. c) MySpace - MySpace was the most visited social networking site in the world from 2005 to 2008 before Facebook's rapid growth overtook it.

5. b) Survivor - "Survivor" premiered on May 31, 2000, and became the most successful summer replacement show in television history, launching the reality TV craze.

6. c) 5 GB - The original iPod could store around 1,000 songs, which was a huge leap at the time and became the basis for its famous marketing slogan.

7. b) 99 - In classic RuneScape, level 99 was the highest achievable level for any skill, becoming a major milestone for players and often celebrated with a "skillcape."

8. a) Red, blue, yellow, green - The original eBay logo used a mix of these four bright colors, making it stand out and feel playful during the early days of online marketplaces.

9. b) Finding Nemo - Released in 2003, Finding Nemo won the Oscar for Best Animated Feature and became one of Pixar's highest-grossing films at the time.

10. b) Kelly Clarkson - Kelly Clarkson won the inaugural season of "American Idol" and launched a successful music career in pop music.

11. c) Twitter - Twitter revolutionized real-time communication and became a major platform for news, politics, and celebrity interaction.

12. b) 2002 - The BlackBerry 5810 was one of the first devices to combine phone functionality with email, marking an important step toward the modern smartphone era.

13. a) The Dark Knight - Released in 2008, it was the second film in Christopher Nolan's Batman trilogy and became one of the highest-grossing and most critically acclaimed superhero films of all time.

14. b) Avatar - James Cameron's "Avatar" became a global phenomenon and held the record for highest-grossing film for nearly a decade.

15. c) Orkut - Orkut was particularly popular in Brazil and India but eventually lost users to Facebook's global expansion.

16. b) Cast Away - "Cast Away" became a massive hit and showcased Tom Hanks' acting range in a survival drama where he was alone for most of the film.

17. c) Xbox Live - Launched in 2002, Xbox Live introduced online multiplayer, voice chat, and digital services to consoles, becoming a major part of Xbox's success in the 2000s.

18. c) 2002 - 8 Mile starred Eminem and became a major hit, with its soundtrack featuring the Oscar-winning song "Lose Yourself."

19. b) Flickr - Flickr launched in 2004 and became hugely popular for sharing photos before Instagram launched and dominated the market.

20. a) Slumdog Millionaire - "Slumdog Millionaire" won the Academy Award for Best Picture in 2009 (for 2008 films) and became a global success.

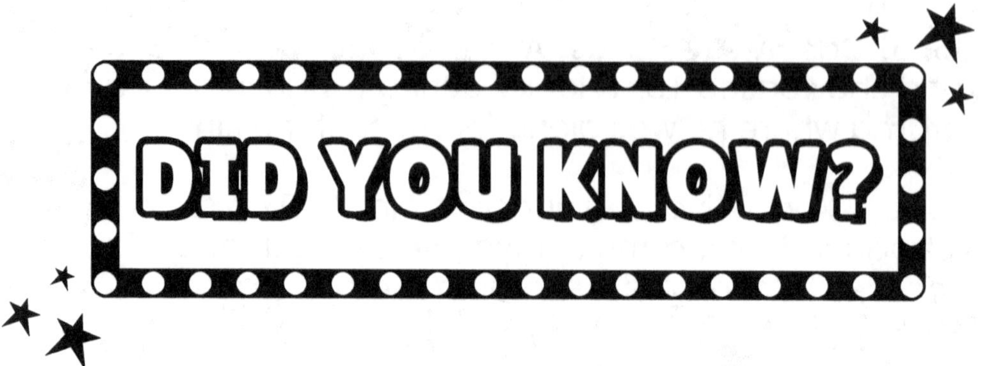

In the early 2000s, texting exploded in popularity, but messages were limited to just 160 characters. Many phones used T9 predictive text, where each number key represented multiple letters, making typing slow and sometimes frustrating. Despite this, texting quickly became one of the main ways people communicated, especially among younger generations.

DVDs replaced VHS tapes faster than most people expected. By the mid-2000s, DVDs made up the majority of home video sales thanks to their better picture quality, bonus features, and the ability to skip directly to scenes. Video rental stores adapted quickly, but within a few years, even DVDs would begin to face competition from digital downloads.

Flash games dominated the internet during this era. Simple browser-based games could be played instantly without downloads, and websites were filled with everything from puzzle games to early multiplayer experiences. Many of these games were created by small developers and became hugely popular, shaping early online gaming culture.

CHAPTER 6

TV & Movie Memories

Television and movies have always been powerful mediums for storytelling, entertainment, and cultural commentary. They transport us to different worlds, introduce us to unforgettable characters, and provide the soundtrack to important moments in our lives. Whether it's a beloved TV show that we watched religiously or a movie that moved us emotionally, these audiovisual experiences shape our memories and define our eras. The greatest shows and films transcend their time, remaining relevant and beloved long after their initial release, and continuing to inspire new generations of viewers.

1. Which TV show aired from 1994 to 2004 and became a cultural phenomenon?

a. Friends
b. Seinfeld
c. Cheers
d. Frasier

2. Which film won the Academy Award for Best Picture in 1995?

a. Forrest Gump
b. Pulp Fiction
c. The Shawshank Redemption
d. Braveheart

3. Which TV show premiered in 1999 and is widely considered one of the greatest TV shows of all time?

a. The Sopranos
b. The Wire
c. Breaking Bad
d. Mad Men

4. Which film became the highest-grossing film of all time until "Avatar" surpassed it in 2010?

a. Titanic
b. Jurassic Park
c. The Lion King
d. E.T.

5. Which TV show premiered in 2004 and became a massive hit with a devoted fanbase?

a. Lost
b. Heroes
c. Prison Break
d. The Office

6. Which film became the highest-grossing film of 2001?

a. Harry Potter and the Philosopher's Stone
b. The Lord of the Rings: The Fellowship of the Ring
c. Monsters, Inc.
d. Pearl Harbor

7. Which TV show premiered in 2011 and became a global phenomenon?

a. Game of Thrones
b. The Walking Dead
c. Breaking Bad
d. Sherlock

8. What is the name of the valuable mineral humans are mining on Pandora in Avatar?

a. Unobtanium
b. Vibranium
c. Tritanium
d. Adamantium

9. Which film won the Academy Award for Best Picture in 2015?

a. Birdman
b. Whiplash
c. The Grand Budapest Hotel
d. Boyhood

10. In Avengers: Endgame, what is the name of the method used by the Avengers to travel through time and collect the Infinity Stones?

a. Quantum Tunneling
b. Multiverse Jumping
c. Quantum Realm time travel
d. Temporal Rift Protocol

11. Which TV show premiered in 2016 and became hugely popular on Netflix?

a. Stranger Things
b. The Crown
c. Ozark
d. Black Mirror

12. Which film became the highest-grossing film of 2023?

a. Barbie
b. Oppenheimer
c. Killers of the Flower Moon
d. The Hunger Games: The Ballad of Songbirds and Snakes

13. Which TV show premiered in 2022 and became one of Netflix's most-watched series?

a. Wednesday
b. Stranger Things Season 4
c. The Midnight Club
d. Lockwood & Co.

14. In The Office, what is the name of the paper company where the characters work?

a. Scranton Paper Co.
b. Dunder Mifflin
c. PaperCorp
d. Penn Paper

15. Which TV show aired from 1993 to 2004 and became one of the most critically acclaimed sitcoms?

a. Frasier
b. Seinfeld
c. Cheers
d. The Mary Tyler Moore Show

16. Which film won the Academy Award for Best Picture in 1996?

a. Braveheart
b. Apollo 13
c. Sense and Sensibility
d. Il Postino

17. Which TV show premiered in 2006 and became one of the most popular dramas of the 2000s?

a. Dexter
b. House
c. The Office
d. 30 Rock

18. Which film became the highest-grossing movie of all time worldwide?

a. Avatar
b. Avengers: Endgame
c. Titanic
d. Star Wars: The Force Awakens

19. Which TV show premiered in 2009 and became hugely popular in the early 2010s?

a. Glee
b. Community
c. Parks and Recreation
d. The Office

20. In Mean Girls, what is the name of the popular girl group that Regina George leads?

a. The Queens
b. The Dolls
c. The Plastics
d. The Elites

CHAPTER 6 ANSWERS

1. a) Friends - "Friends" aired from 1994 to 2004 and became a cultural phenomenon that defined the 1990s and 2000s with its relatable characters and humor.

2. a) Forrest Gump - "Forrest Gump" won the Academy Award for Best Picture in 1995 (for 1994 films) with Tom Hanks in an iconic role.

3. a) The Sopranos - "The Sopranos" premiered in 1999 and is widely considered one of the greatest TV shows of all time, revolutionizing what television drama could be.

4. a) Titanic - "Titanic" became the highest-grossing film of all time until "Avatar" surpassed it in 2010, holding the record for nearly 12 years.

5. a) Lost - "Lost" premiered in 2004 and became a massive hit, spawning countless imitators and fan theories about its mysterious plot.

6. a) Harry Potter and the Philosopher's Stone - "Harry Potter and the Philosopher's Stone" became the highest-grossing film of 2001 and launched a franchise.

7. a) Game of Thrones - "Game of Thrones" premiered in 2011 and became a global phenomenon that dominated television for nearly a decade.

8. a) Unobtanium - The rare and extremely valuable mineral "Unobtanium" is the main reason humans are on Pandora, driving the conflict at the center of the film.

9. a) Birdman - "Birdman" won the Academy Award for Best Picture in 2015 (for 2014 films) with Michael Keaton in a career-defining role.

10. c) Quantum Realm time travel - The Avengers use the Quantum Realm, along with Pym Particles, to travel through time and retrieve the Infinity Stones in different points of the past.

11. a) Stranger Things - "Stranger Things" premiered in 2016 and became hugely popular on Netflix with its nostalgic 1980s setting.

12. a) Barbie - "Barbie" became the highest-grossing film of 2023 and a cultural phenomenon with Margot Robbie in the lead role.

13. a) Wednesday - "Wednesday" premiered in 2022 and became one of Netflix's most-watched series with Jenna Ortega in the lead role.

14. b) Dunder Mifflin - The show is set at the Scranton branch of Dunder Mifflin, and its quirky employees are at the center of the series' humor.

15. a) Frasier - "Frasier" aired from 1993 to 2004 and became one of the most critically acclaimed sitcoms of the 1990s and 2000s.

16. a) Braveheart - "Braveheart" won the Academy Award for Best Picture in 1996 (for 1995 films) with Mel Gibson directing and starring.

17. a) Dexter - "Dexter" premiered in 2006 and became one of the most popular dramas of the 2000s with Michael C. Hall in the lead role.

18. a) Avatar - Originally released in 2009, "Avatar" became the highest-grossing film of all time, later reclaiming the top spot after re-releases, surpassing "Avengers: Endgame."

19. a) Glee - "Glee" premiered in 2009 and became hugely popular in the early 2010s with its musical performances and ensemble cast.

20. c) The Plastics - The Plastics are the most popular clique in the school, known for their strict rules, iconic quotes, and influence over the social hierarchy.

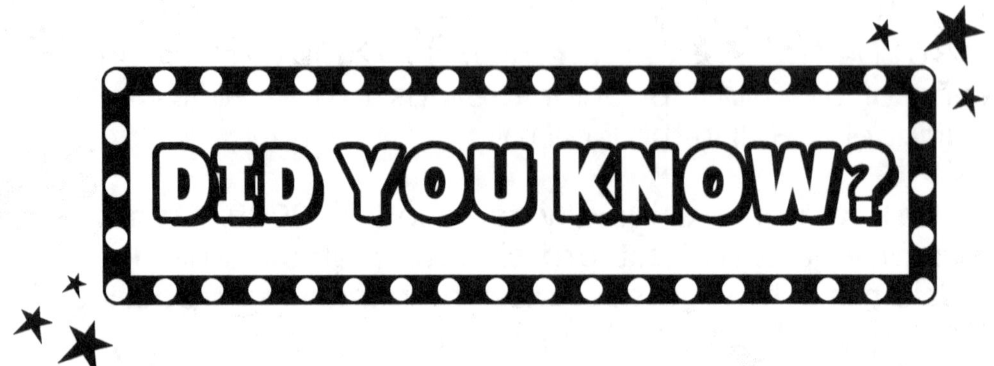

Binge-watching wasn't always a thing. Before streaming, most TV shows released one episode per week, and if you missed it, you often had to wait for a rerun or hope someone recorded it. This made finales and cliffhangers huge events, with millions watching at the same time. People would talk about episodes the next day at school or work, and spoilers were a real concern even without social media.

Movie trailers used to be shown after the film, not before it. That's where the name "trailer" comes from, since they originally trailed the main feature. Studios eventually moved them to the beginning so audiences wouldn't leave early. Today, trailers are major events themselves, sometimes watched millions of times online before a movie is even released.

Laugh tracks in sitcoms often used the same recordings for decades. Some of the laughter heard in shows today was originally recorded in the 1950s, meaning you might be hearing reactions from audiences who watched completely different shows. This technique helped make scenes feel funnier and more engaging, even when no live audience was present.

CHAPTER 7

The Digital Revolution

The period from 2010 to 2014 represented a pivotal moment in the digital revolution. Smartphones were becoming ubiquitous, social media platforms were exploding in popularity, and the internet was becoming faster and more accessible than ever before. This was the era when Instagram launched and became a global phenomenon, when Snapchat introduced disappearing messages, and when Netflix began its transformation from a DVD rental service to a streaming giant. The digital revolution that had been building since the 1990s finally reached critical mass during this period, fundamentally transforming how we communicate, consume media, and share our lives with others.

1. Which social media platform launched in October 2010 and became a global phenomenon?

a. Snapchat
b. Instagram
c. Pinterest
d. Vine

2. In what year did iPad first launch, helping to popularize modern tablet computing?

a. 2007
b. 2009
c. 2010
d. 2012

3. Which operating system did the original Samsung Galaxy S run when it was first released?

a. Symbian
b. Windows Mobile
c. Android
d. Bada

4. In Vine, how long could a single video clip be?

a. 5 seconds
b. 6 seconds
c. 10 seconds
d. 15 seconds

5. In the original Snapchat logo (the ghost known as "Ghostface Chillah"), which eye is shown winking?

a. Left eye
b. Right eye
c. Both eyes
d. Neither eye

6. What was the name of Apple's music service that was replaced by Apple Music in 2015?

a. iTunes Radio
b. Apple Beats
c. iMusic
d. SoundCloud

7. Which movie starring Robert Downey Jr. was released in 2012 and became a massive hit?

a. Iron Man
b. The Avengers
c. Iron Man 3
d. Captain America: The Winter Soldier

8. Which video game was released by Activision in 2012?

a. Call of Duty: Black Ops II
b. Call of Duty: Modern Warfare 3
c. Call of Duty: Ghosts
d. Call of Duty: Advanced Warfare

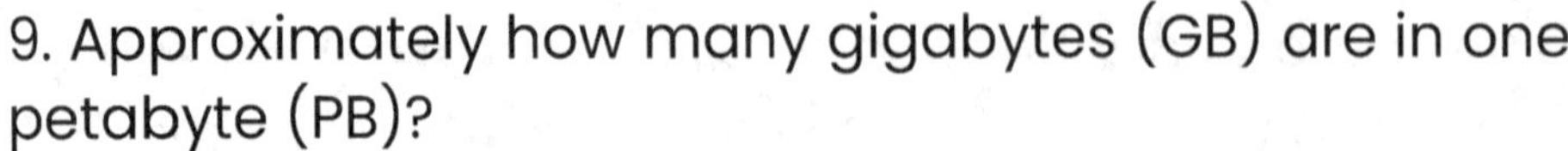

9. Approximately how many gigabytes (GB) are in one petabyte (PB)?

a. 100,000
b. 500,000
c. 1,000,000
d. 10,000,000

10. What does "HTTP" stand for in a website address like http://?

a. Hyperlink Transfer Text Protocol
b. High Text Transfer Protocol
c. Hypertext Transfer Protocol
d. Hypertext Transmission Process

11. Which early social media platform allowed users to submit links that could be upvoted to reach its front page, heavily influencing internet trends in the mid-2000s?

a. Reddit
b. Pinterest
c. StumbleUpon
d. Digg

12. Which music streaming service was acquired by Apple in 2014?

a. Spotify
b. Beats Music
c. Rdio
d. MOG

13. What was the name of the viral challenge that became famous in 2014?

a. Ice Bucket Challenge
b. Mannequin Challenge
c. Bottle Flip Challenge
d. Tide Pod Challenge

14. Which video game was released in 2013 and became hugely popular?

a. Grand Theft Auto V
b. The Last of Us
c. Bioshock Infinite
d. All of the above

15. In what year did Apple Watch first launch?

a. 2013
b. 2014
c. 2015
d. 2016

16. In Pokémon GO, what item is used to attract Pokémon to a specific location for a limited time?

a. Incense
b. Poké Ball
c. Lure Module
d. Lucky Egg

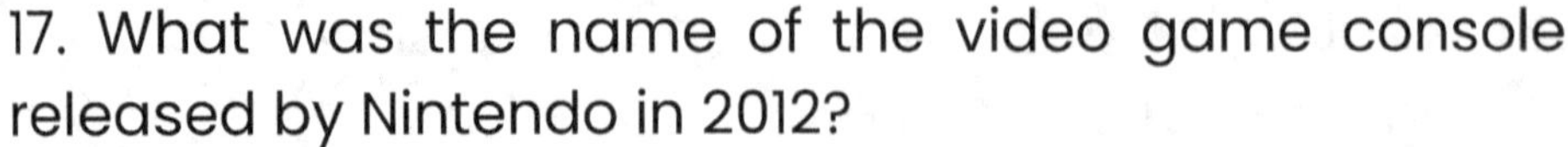

17. What was the name of the video game console released by Nintendo in 2012?

a. Wii U
b. Nintendo Switch
c. GameCube
d. Wii

18. What does the "MP" stand for in a camera specification like 12MP?

a. Mega Pixels
b. Mega Points
c. Micro Pixels
d. Multi Pixels

19. What does the "Wi-Fi" in wireless internet actually stand for?

a. Wireless Fidelity
b. Wide Frequency
c. Wireless Frequency Interface
d. It doesn't officially stand for anything

20. What does "PDF" stand for in a file format like a document download?

a. Personal Document File
b. Portable Data File
c. Printed Document Format
d. Portable Document Format

CHAPTER 7 ANSWERS

1. b) Instagram - Instagram launched in October 2010 and grew to one million users within two months, becoming a cultural phenomenon that changed how people share photos.

2. c) 2010 - The first iPad was released in 2010, creating a new mainstream market for tablets and bridging the gap between smartphones and laptops.

3. c) Android - The original Galaxy S ran Android, helping Samsung compete directly with Apple's iPhone and marking the beginning of its dominance in the smartphone market.

4. b) 6 seconds - Vine limited videos to six seconds, which led to fast, creative, and often looping content that defined early short-form video culture.

5. a) Left eye - In early versions of the Snapchat logo, the ghost character was shown winking its left eye, a small detail many users remember from the app's early days.

6. a) iTunes Radio - Apple launched iTunes Radio in 2013 as a streaming service, but it was later discontinued and replaced by Apple Music in 2015 as the company shifted to a full subscription model.

7. b) The Avengers - "The Avengers" became the highest-grossing film of 2012 and launched the Marvel Cinematic Universe into the stratosphere.

8. a) Call of Duty: Black Ops II – "Call of Duty: Black Ops II" was one of the best-selling games of the generation in 2012.

9. c) 1,000,000 – One petabyte equals about 1 million gigabytes, showing just how massive modern data storage has become.

10. c) Hypertext Transfer Protocol – HTTP is the foundational protocol used for transmitting web pages across the internet.

11. d) Digg – Digg was known for its front-page system where user-submitted links could go viral based on votes, making it one of the most influential sites for online content discovery in the mid-2000s.

12. b) Beats Music – Apple acquired Beats Music (along with Beats Electronics) for 3 billion dollars in 2014.

13. a) Ice Bucket Challenge - The Ice Bucket Challenge became a global phenomenon in 2014, raising awareness and funds for ALS research.

14. d) All of the above - 2013 was an exceptional year for video game releases with multiple major titles hitting the market.

15. c) 2015 – The Apple Watch was released in 2015, marking Apple's entry into wearable technology and integrating health tracking, notifications, and apps into a smartwatch.

16. c) Lure Module – Lures are placed on PokéStops to attract Pokémon for all nearby players, making them a key social feature of the game.

17. a) Wii U - The Wii U was released by Nintendo in 2012 as the successor to the Wii with a tablet controller.

18. a) Mega Pixels - MP stands for megapixels, representing one million pixels and commonly used to measure the resolution of digital cameras and smartphone photos.

19. d) It doesn't officially stand for anything - Despite the common belief that it means "Wireless Fidelity," Wi-Fi is simply a brand name and doesn't have an official full form.

20. d) Portable Document Format - PDF files were designed to preserve formatting across devices, making them one of the most widely used document formats in the digital world.

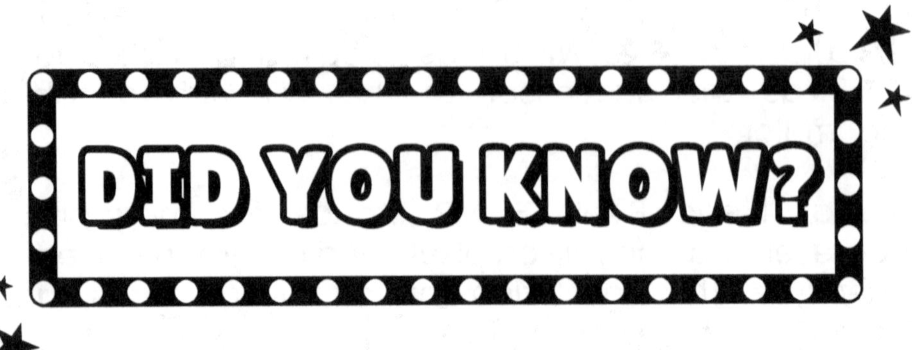

Selfies became a global trend during this period, but the word "selfie" was actually named the Word of the Year in 2013. Front-facing cameras made it easier than ever to take photos of yourself, and social media turned it into a cultural habit. What started as a simple self-photo quickly became a major part of online identity and personal branding.

Streaming began to replace downloads faster than expected. Instead of buying songs or movies, people started paying monthly subscriptions for unlimited access. This shift changed how entertainment was valued, with convenience becoming more important than ownership for the first time.

App stores exploded in popularity, with millions of apps available within just a few years. Some of the simplest ideas became massive hits, with games and tools downloaded hundreds of millions of times. It showed that anyone with a good idea could reach a global audience almost instantly.

CHAPTER 8

Pop Culture Phenomena & Social Media

Pop culture has always been a reflection of society, capturing the zeitgeist of an era and providing commentary on the issues and trends that define our time. From celebrity gossip to viral memes, from award show moments to social media trends, pop culture is the shared language that connects us across generations and cultures. The rise of social media has fundamentally changed pop culture, democratizing who gets to be famous and giving ordinary people the ability to become celebrities overnight. What was once controlled by major media companies is now created, shared, and discussed by millions of people on social media platforms.

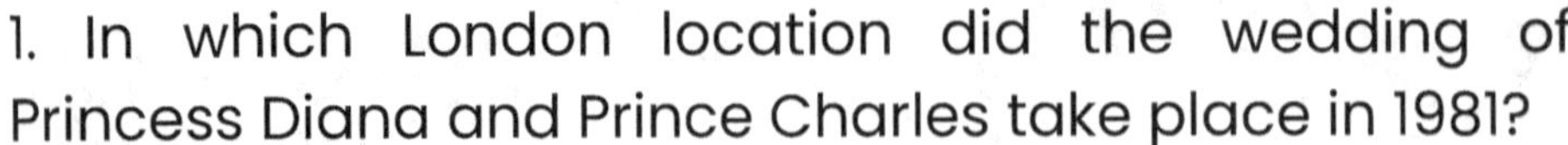

1. In which London location did the wedding of Princess Diana and Prince Charles take place in 1981?

a. St Paul's Cathedral
b. Westminster Abbey
c. Buckingham Palace
d. Windsor Castle

2. In most Harlem Shake videos, what item was commonly worn by the first person dancing before the beat drop?

a. Sunglasses
b. A mask or helmet
c. A suit
d. Headphones

3. Which network originally aired Keeping Up with the Kardashians when it premiered in 2007?

a. MTV
b. VH1
c. Bravo
d. E!

4. What was the name of the viral video that became famous in 2012?

a. "Gangnam Style"
b. "Harlem Shake"
c. "Charlie Bit My Finger"
d. "Numa Numa"

5. Which celebrity couple's breakup dominated headlines in 2016?

a. Brad Pitt and Angelina Jolie
b. Johnny Depp and Amber Heard
c. Ben Affleck and Jennifer Garner
d. Gwen Stefani and Gavin Rossdale

6. What was the name of the meme that became famous in 2015?

a. Harambe
b. The Dress
c. Doge
d. Damn Daniel

7. Which award show had a famous incident in 2022?

a. The Oscars
b. The Grammys
c. The Golden Globes
d. The Emmys

8. What was the name of the blog that became famous in the mid-2000s for posting celebrity gossip with red scribbles over photos?

a. TMZ
b. BuzzFeed
c. Gawker
d. Perez Hilton

9. On which platform did Old Town Road first go viral in 2019?

a. Instagram
b. YouTube
c. TikTok
d. Twitter

10. Which celebrity became famous for her TikTok videos in 2020?

a. Charli D'Amelio
b. Addison Rae
c. Zoe Laverne
d. Dixie D'Amelio

11. What was the name of the popular mobile drawing game released in 2012 where players guessed each other's sketches?

a) Words With Friends
b) Draw Something
c) Sketch It
d) Guess Draw

12. Which celebrity became famous for her role in "Wednesday" in 2022?

a. Jenna Ortega
b. Emma Myers
c. Luyanda Unati Lewis-Nyawo
d. Hunter Doohan

13. What was the original name of TikTok before it was rebranded globally in 2018?

a. Musical
b. Music.ly
c. Musical.ly
d. Vine

14. Which company owns Twitch, the platform that became hugely popular for live streaming video games?

a. Google
b. Meta
c. Microsoft
d. Amazon

15. What was the original name of Instagram during its early development phase before launch in 2010?

a. PicShare
b. Burbn
c. SnapPic
d. PhotoGram

16. What was the name of the mobile game released in 2013 that became infamous for its extreme difficulty and simple tapping mechanic?

a) Crossy Road
b) Flappy Bird
c) Jetpack Joyride
d) Tiny Wings

17. What was the name of the meme that became famous in 2016?

a. Harambe
b. The Dress
c. Doge
d. Damn Daniel

18. What was the title of the first-ever video uploaded to YouTube in 2005?

a. First Video Ever
b. Zoo Visit
c. Me at the zoo
d. My First Clip

19. What was the name of the YouTube video that became the first to reach 1 billion views?

a. Baby
b. Gangnam Style
c. Despacito
d. See You Again

20. Which dance move from Fortnite became a global craze among kids and athletes?

a. The Shuffle
b. The Dab
c. The Floss
d. The Twist

CHAPTER 8 ANSWERS

1. a) St Paul's Cathedral - Unlike most royal weddings, which are held at Westminster Abbey, Charles and Diana's ceremony took place at St Paul's Cathedral to accommodate the massive global audience and guest list.

2. b) A mask or helmet - The first dancer was often masked (like a helmet or costume), adding to the randomness before the chaos kicked in.

3. d) E! - The show premiered on the E! network, which was known for celebrity-focused programming and helped build the Kardashian brand.

4. a) "Gangnam Style" - "Gangnam Style" by PSY became a global phenomenon in 2012 with its viral dance moves.

5. a) Brad Pitt and Angelina Jolie - Brad Pitt and Angelina Jolie's breakup dominated headlines in 2016 with celebrity gossip.

6. b) The Dress - "The Dress" became a viral sensation in 2015 when people debated whether it was blue and black or white and gold.

7. a) The Oscars - Will Smith slapped Chris Rock at the 2022 Academy Awards, becoming one of the most talked-about moments in Oscar history.

8. d) Perez Hilton - The blog became hugely popular for its messy, hand-drawn annotations on paparazzi photos, defining early internet celebrity gossip culture.

9. c) TikTok - "Old Town Road" exploded in popularity through TikTok trends and memes before becoming a global chart-topping hit.

10. a) Charli D'Amelio - Charli D'Amelio became the most-followed person on TikTok with millions of followers.

11. b) Draw Something – Released in 2012, it became a viral hit by turning a classic drawing game into a social mobile experience.

12. a) Jenna Ortega - Jenna Ortega became a star after her role in Netflix's "Wednesday" with her iconic dance scene.

13. c) Musical.ly – The app was originally called Musical.ly before being acquired and merged into TikTok, making it a key part of its global rise.

14. d) Amazon - Amazon acquired Twitch in 2014, helping it grow into the dominant platform for gaming streams and esports content.

15. b) Burbn - Instagram began as a location-based check-in app called Burbn before pivoting to focus on photo sharing, which led to its massive success.

16. b) Flappy Bird – Released in 2013, it went viral for its frustrating gameplay before being suddenly removed by its creator despite huge success.

17. a) Harambe - Harambe the gorilla became a viral meme in 2016 after his death at the Cincinnati Zoo.

18. c) Me at the zoo – The first YouTube video, uploaded by co-founder Jawed Karim, showed him at the San Diego Zoo and has since become a piece of internet history.

19. b) Gangnam Style – Gangnam Style became the first YouTube video to surpass 1 billion views, marking a major milestone in internet and pop culture history.

20. c) The Floss – Popularized by Fortnite and social media, it became a worldwide trend.

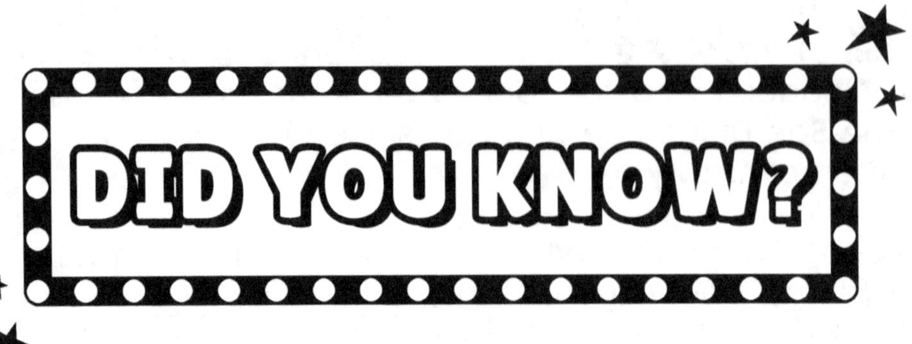

Going viral was not always instant. In the early days of the internet, videos and memes spread through emails, forums, and word of mouth, sometimes taking weeks or even months to reach a large audience. People would share links manually, and there were no algorithms pushing content to millions. Today, a single post can reach global audiences within hours, completely changing how quickly trends and moments take off.

Hashtags were not originally created for social media. The "#" symbol was first used in telephone systems in the 1970s, but it was later adopted online to help group conversations together. It eventually became a key part of platforms like Twitter and Instagram, allowing users to follow trends, join discussions, and make content more discoverable across the world.

Influencers as we know them today did not exist before social media. In the past, fame was controlled by television, movies, and music industries, but digital platforms allowed everyday people to build massive followings. Some creators started by posting simple content from their bedrooms and went on to earn millions through brand deals, completely reshaping what it means to be famous.

The Streaming Age & Modern Era

The period from 2015 to 2026 represents the era of streaming dominance, where digital content has become the primary way we consume entertainment. Netflix, which started as a DVD rental service, has become a global entertainment powerhouse with original content that rivals traditional studios. Streaming services like Disney+, Apple TV+, and HBO Max have launched and become major players in the entertainment landscape. Meanwhile, platforms like Spotify have fundamentally changed how we listen to music, and social media platforms like TikTok have created new forms of entertainment and celebrity.

1. What is the name of the fictional town where Stranger Things is set?

a. Hawkins
b. Riverdale
c. Sunnydale
d. Hill Valley

2. In Spotify, what was the original name of the feature now known as "Discover Weekly" during its internal testing phase?

a. Taste Profile
b. Music Match
c. Playlist AI
d. Weekly Mix

3. Which streaming service first released the series House of Cards in 2013, marking a major shift toward original content?

a. Hulu
b. Amazon Prime Video
c. Netflix
d. HBO Max

4. Which 2017 video game introduced the "Battle Royale" mode that helped it become a global cultural phenomenon?

a. PlayerUnknown's Battlegrounds
b. Fortnite
c. Call of Duty: WWII
d. Apex Legends

5. Which streaming service launched in 2019 and competed with Netflix?

a. Disney+
b. Apple TV+
c. HBO Max
d. Peacock

6. What is the name of the child character in The Mandalorian who became a viral pop culture phenomenon?

a. Grogu
b. Yaddle
c. Yoda Jr.
d. The Child

7. What technology underpins cryptocurrencies like Bitcoin?

a. Cloud computing
b. Machine learning
c. Blockchain
d. Data mining

8. On Twitch, what is the name of the monthly paid feature that allows viewers to support a streamer and unlock perks?

a. Channel Membership
b. Twitch Sub
c. Stream Subscription
d. Subscriber Tier

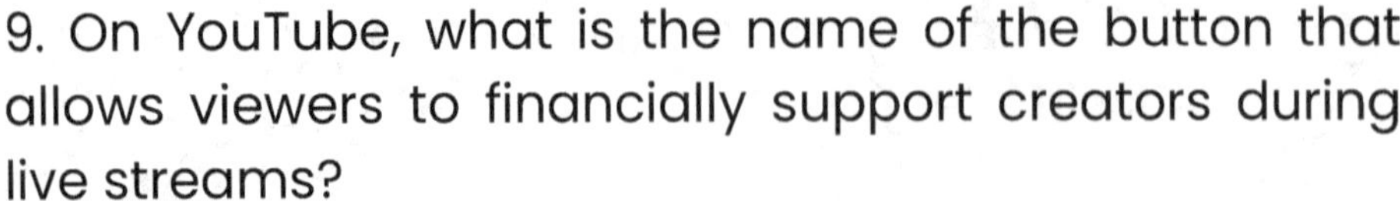

9. On YouTube, what is the name of the button that allows viewers to financially support creators during live streams?

a. Tip
b. Donate
c. Super Like
d. Super Chat

10. What does "GPT" stand for in ChatGPT?

a. General Processing Technology
b. Generated Program Text
c. Global Prediction Tool
d. Generative Pre-trained Transformer

11. What is the name of the feature on TikTok that allows videos to be discovered by a wide audience through its recommendation algorithm?

a. Discover Feed
b. Trending Page
c. Explore
d. For You Page

12. How is "engagement rate" typically calculated for social media content?

a. Likes ÷ followers
b. Views ÷ followers
c. (Likes + comments + shares) ÷ total followers
d. Followers ÷ total posts

13. In what year did Netflix first introduce its streaming service?

a. 2005
b. 2007
c. 2009
d. 2011

14. In what year was Bitcoin first introduced?

a. 2007
b. 2008
c. 2009
d. 2010

15. What was the name of the website that eventually became Twitch?

a. StreamHub
b. Justin.tv
c. LiveCast
d. GameStream

16. Which film won the Academy Award for Best Picture in 2020?

a. Parasite
b. 1917
c. Once Upon a Time in Hollywood
d. Joker

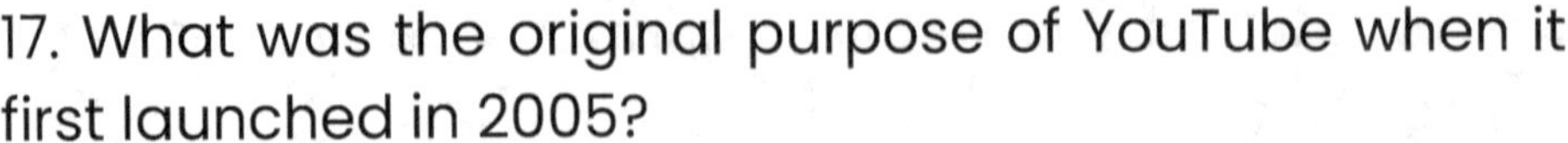

17. What was the original purpose of YouTube when it first launched in 2005?

a. Music streaming
b. Online dating videos
c. Video sharing for any content
d. Live streaming

18. Which streaming service released the hit series "The Rings of Power" in 2022?

a. Netflix
b. Amazon Prime Video
c. Disney+
d. Apple TV+

19. What was the original character limit on Twitter before it doubled?

a. 100
b. 120
c. 140
d. 160

20. What was the original focus of Instagram before it pivoted?

a. Messaging
b. Check-ins and location sharing
c. Video streaming
d. Blogging

1. a) Hawkins - The series takes place in Hawkins, Indiana, a small town where the supernatural events of the show unfold.

2. a) Taste Profile - Spotify initially referred to its recommendation system as "Taste Profile," which later evolved into features like Discover Weekly that personalize music suggestions for users.

3. c) Netflix - House of Cards was one of the first major original series from a streaming platform, signaling a turning point in how TV content was produced and consumed.

4. b) Fortnite - Although PUBG popularized the genre, Fortnite's free-to-play Battle Royale mode and constant updates turned it into a massive global hit.

5. a) Disney+ - Disney+ launched in November 2019 and immediately became a major player in the streaming wars with content.

6. a) Grogu - Although initially referred to as "The Child" or "Baby Yoda," the character's real name, Grogu, was later revealed and became widely known among fans.

7. c) Blockchain - Blockchain is a decentralized ledger system that records transactions securely across many computers.

8. b) Twitch Sub - Commonly referred to as a "sub," this feature lets viewers support streamers monthly while gaining access to perks like emotes and badges.

9. d) Super Chat - Super Chat lets viewers pay to highlight their messages during live streams, becoming a popular way to support creators and stand out in chat.

10. d) Generative Pre-trained Transformer - GPT refers to a type of AI model trained on large amounts of data to generate human-like text.

11. d) For You Page - Often called the "FYP," this feed uses TikTok's algorithm to show users personalized content, playing a huge role in viral trends.

12. c) (Likes + comments + shares) ÷ total followers - Engagement rate measures how actively an audience interacts with content relative to the size of the account.

13. b) 2007 - Netflix launched streaming as "Watch Now," marking the beginning of the shift from DVDs to digital entertainment.

14. c) 2009 - Bitcoin was launched in 2009 by the pseudonymous creator Satoshi Nakamoto, marking the beginning of cryptocurrency as a global phenomenon.

15. b) Justin.tv - Twitch originally started as Justin.tv in 2007, a platform for live streaming everyday life before evolving into a gaming-focused service.

16. a) Parasite - "Parasite" won Best Picture in 2020 (for 2019 films), marking the first non-English language film to win.

17. c) Video sharing for any content – YouTube was created as a simple platform where users could upload, watch, and share videos of any kind, making online video accessible to everyone.

18. b) Amazon Prime Video - "The Rings of Power" became one of Amazon Prime Video's most popular series in 2022.

19. c) 140 - The limit was based on SMS constraints before increasing to 280 characters.

20. b) Check-ins and location sharing - Instagram started as Burbn, a location-based app before focusing on photos.

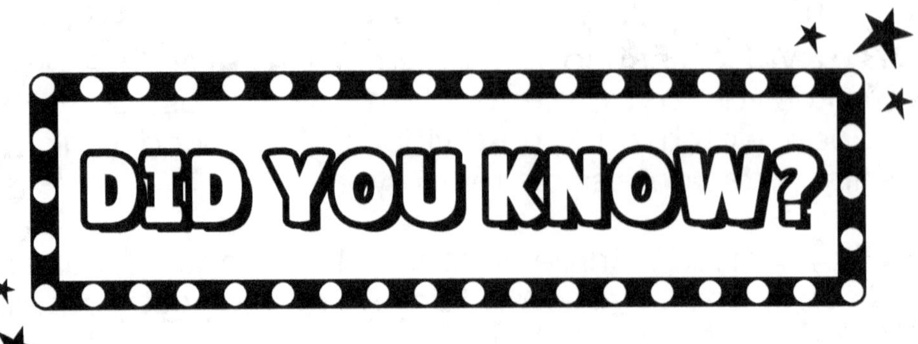

Streaming changed not just how we watch, but how shows are made. Entire seasons are now released at once, encouraging binge-watching, which has influenced storytelling with more cliffhangers and faster pacing. Some shows are even written knowing viewers might watch multiple episodes in one sitting rather than waiting week to week.

Algorithms now play a major role in what people watch and listen to. Platforms study viewing habits, watch time, and even when users stop watching to recommend content. This means two people on the same app can have completely different homepages, each tailored to their personal tastes without them even realizing it.

Short-form content has reshaped attention spans. Videos that are just seconds long can reach millions of people, and creators often aim to capture attention within the first few seconds. This has changed not only entertainment, but also how brands, influencers, and even news outlets communicate online.

CHAPTER 10

Say What? Slang, Ads & Catchphrases

Language is constantly evolving, reflecting the times we live in and the values we hold. Slang is the cutting edge of language evolution, where new words and phrases emerge to describe new experiences, technologies, and social phenomena. From "rad" and "tubular" in the 1990s to "lit" and "fire" in the 2010s to "sus" and "no cap" in the 2020s, slang captures the spirit of each generation and provides a window into how young people think and communicate. Advertising, meanwhile, has always been a reflection of cultural values and aspirations, with iconic slogans and campaigns becoming part of our collective memory.

1. Which brand used the slogan "Snap! Crackle! Pop!"?

a. Cornflakes
b. Cheerios
c. Rice Krispies
d. Frosted Flakes

2. Which brand used the slogan "Is It In You?"

a. Powerade
b. Red Bull
c. Gatorade
d. Monster

3. Which brand used the slogan "Betcha Can't Eat Just One"?

a. Doritos
b. Lay's
c. Pringles
d. Cheetos

4. What was the name of the advertising campaign that became famous in 1993?

a. "Got Milk?"
b. "Where's the Beef?"
c. "I'm Lovin' It"
d. "Think Different"

5. Which company used the slogan "Obey Your Thirst"?

a. Coca-Cola
b. Gatorade
c. Pepsi
d. Sprite

6. What was the name of the advertising slogan used by Apple in 1997?

a. "Think Different"
b. "Just Do It"
c. "Have It Your Way"
d. "I'm Lovin' It"

7. Which slang term became popular in the 1980s to describe something cool?

a. Awesome
b. Radical
c. Tubular
d. Gnarly

8. What does "ROFL" stand for?

a. Rolling On Floor Laughing
b. Running Out For Lunch
c. Really Odd Funny Line
d. Rolling On Funny Laughs

9. What does "WB" mean in MSN conversations?

a. Write Back
b. Welcome Back
c. Wait Briefly
d. Watch Back

10. Which brand used the slogan "Think Small"?

a. Ford
b. Toyota
c. Volkswagen
d. Honda

11. Which slang term became especially popular in the late 1990s, particularly in hip-hop culture, to describe something stylish, impressive, or excellent?

a. Dope
b. Lit
c. Yeet
d. Bussin

12. Which company used the slogan "Because You're Worth It"?

a. Maybelline
b. Revlon
c. L'Oréal
d. CoverGirl

13. What was the name of the advertising campaign that became famous in 1984?

a. "Just Do It"
b. "Think Different"
c. "Where's the Beef?"
d. "Have It Your Way"

14. Which brand used the slogan "I Am What I Am"?

a. Nike
b. Adidas
c. Reebok
d. New Balance

15. Which slang term became popular in the 2000s to describe something uncool or lame?

a. Wack
b. Lame
c. Whack
d. Weak

16. Which artist performed the jingle for the "I'm Lovin' It" campaign used by McDonald's?

a. Usher
b. Pharrell Williams
c. Justin Timberlake
d. Nelly

17. What does "NPC" stand for?

a. Non-Playable Character
b. New Player Class
c. Non-Primary Character
d. Neutral Player Code

18. What does "smurfing" mean in competitive games?

a. Playing with friends
b. Using a lower-level account to play against weaker opponents
c. Switching teams mid-game
d. Sharing accounts

19. The slang term "sus," which became widely popular in the 2020s, gained mainstream usage through which online game?

a. Among Us
b. Fortnite
c. Call of Duty: Warzone
d. Minecraft

20. What does "GG EZ" imply in online gaming?

a. Good Game, Easy
b. Good Game, Excellent
c. Get Good, Easy
d. Game Gone Easy

CHAPTER 10 ANSWERS

1. c) Rice Krispies - The slogan refers to the cereal's sound when milk is added.

2. c) Gatorade - This campaign focused on performance and inner drive.

3. b) Lay's - This slogan emphasized the addictive nature of the chips.

4. a) "Got Milk?" - The "Got Milk?" campaign became one of the most iconic advertising campaigns of all time in 1993.

5. d) Sprite - A defining campaign of the 1990s focused on authenticity.

6. a) "Think Different" - Apple's "Think Different" campaign became one of the most iconic advertising campaigns of all time.

7. c) Tubular - "Tubular" became popular slang in the 1980s to describe something cool or awesome.

8. a) Rolling On Floor Laughing - An exaggerated version of LOL.

9. b) Welcome Back - Often used when someone returned after being AFK.

10. c) Volkswagen - This campaign from the 1960s revolutionized advertising by embracing simplicity and humility.

11. a) Dope – "Dope" was widely used throughout the 1990s, especially in hip-hop culture, to describe something cool, impressive, or high quality.

12. c) L'Oréal - A powerful slogan emphasizing self-worth and empowerment.

13. c) "Where's the Beef?" - Wendy's "Where's the Beef?" campaign became iconic in the 1980s as a memorable advertising moment.

14. c) Reebok - This campaign focused on individuality and self-expression, becoming one of Reebok's most recognizable slogans.

15. d) Weak - Multiple slang terms were used in the 2000s to describe something uncool or lame.

16. c) Justin Timberlake - He performed the "I'm Lovin' It" jingle in 2003 as part of McDonald's global advertising campaign, helping make the slogan iconic.

17. a) Non-Playable Character - Characters controlled by the game rather than players.

18. b) Using a lower-level account to play against weaker opponents - Done to dominate easier matches.

19. a) Among Us - The game's social deduction gameplay, where players had to identify the "impostor," made the term "sus" (short for suspicious) explode in popularity and spread into mainstream slang.

20. a) Good Game, Easy - Often used sarcastically or disrespectfully after a win.

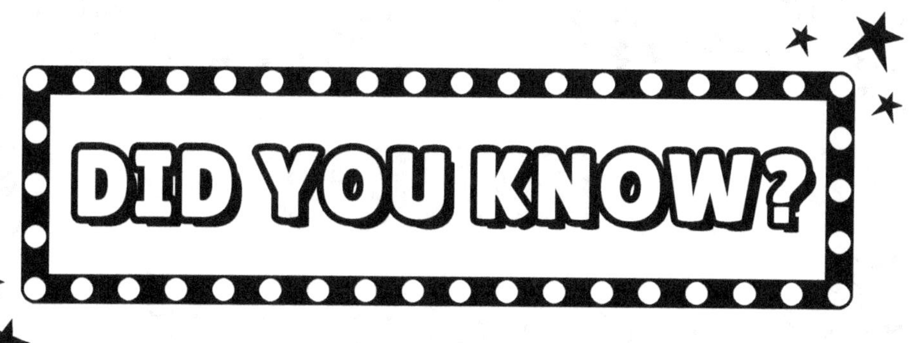

In the past, trends and ideas moved at a much slower pace. Slang terms often took years to spread beyond their original communities, traveling through music, movies, and everyday conversations. Advertising followed a similar pattern, relying heavily on repetition, catchy jingles, and bold slogans because there were fewer ways to reach an audience. With limited TV channels and no social media, brands focused on being memorable enough to stick in people's minds. At the same time, everyday expenses reflected a different lifestyle, things like long-distance phone calls, CDs, and even internet access could feel like premium costs rather than basic necessities.

Today, everything moves faster and feels far more connected. A single viral video, meme, or trend can introduce a new slang term to millions of people within hours, making language spread almost instantly across the world. Advertising has also evolved, shifting toward content that feels more natural and relatable, often blending seamlessly into social media feeds instead of standing out as obvious commercials. Meanwhile, the way we spend money has changed just as dramatically. Many things that once required separate purchases are now bundled into subscriptions, while new digital expenses, like streaming platforms, apps, and online services, have become part of everyday life. The result is a world where culture, communication, and spending habits all evolve faster than ever before.

Some of the best moments of the last 30 years were not headlines. They were your memories. The songs you had on repeat, the late nights with friends, the small moments that stuck with you. Take a few minutes to write them down. You might be surprised by what comes back.

Your First Phone

Was it a flip phone, slider, or your first smartphone? Did it have Snake? Custom ringtones? Who was the first person you texted?

____

____

____

Your First Social Media Account

Was it MSN, MySpace, Facebook, or something else? What was your profile like? Do you remember your first status or username?

____

____

____

Your First Big Purchase

What was the first thing you saved up for? A phone, a console, clothes, or something else? Why did it feel so important at the time?

____

____

____

Your First Concert or Festival

Who did you see? Where was it? Do you remember the ticket price? What was the vibe like?

____

____

____

The Biggest World Event You Remember

Where were you when it happened? Who were you with? How did it make you feel?

____

____

____

The Best App or Invention in Your Lifetime

What changed your daily life the most? Social media? Smartphones? Streaming? Why did it matter to you?

____

____

____

The Most Embarrassing Trend You Followed

Frosted tips? Facebook pokes? Duck-face selfies? What did you wear or do that makes you laugh now?

____

____

____

Your Teenage Weekend Routine

What did a typical weekend look like? Who were you with? What did you do? Gaming, parties, movies, hanging out?

____

____

____

CONCLUSION

As you close this book, it's clear that the last 30 years have been anything but ordinary. From dial-up internet to smartphones, from DVDs to streaming, from playground memories to global moments we all shared, this has been a lifetime shaped by constant change and unforgettable experiences.

But beyond the trivia, the real story is yours.

The songs you played on repeat. The shows you never missed. The trends you followed. The people you laughed with. The moments that didn't make headlines but meant everything to you. These are the memories that truly define your generation.

Turning 30 isn't about looking back with nostalgia alone. It's about recognizing how much you've experienced, how much the world has changed around you, and how much is still ahead.

So whether you aced the quiz or guessed your way through, hopefully this book reminded you of just how much you've lived, seen, and been a part of.

And the best part?

You're only just getting started.

Thanks for Reading!

Thanks for picking up this book! As a special thank-you, I've lined up some awesome freebies for you:

• 500 World War I & II Facts — digital edition
• 101 Idioms and Phrases — digital edition
• 1,144 Random Facts — full audiobook

Scan the QR code below, enter your email, and all three bonuses will be on their way. Enjoy your extra content!